TABLE OF CONTENTS

..... 5
SIDNEY CROSBY 6
DREW DOUGHTY 9
CLAUDE GIROUX 10
ERIK KARLSSON 13
EVGENI MALKIN 14
ALEX OVECHKIN 17
ZACH PARISE 18
CAREY PRICE 21
JONATHAN QUICK 22
STEVEN STAMKOS ... 25
JOHN TAVARES 26
JONATHAN TOEWS 29
SHEA WEBER ... 30
RISING STARS ... 32
READ MORE 32
INTERNET SITES 32
INDEX .....

From teenage phenoms to college-age Stanley Cup winners, young players have made a big impact on the National Hockey League. In just a few years as professionals, some of the best are skating their way toward legendary careers.

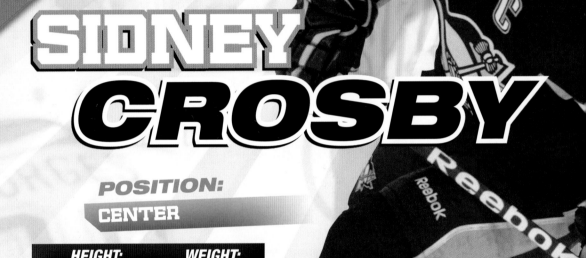

SIDNEY CROSBY

POSITION:

CENTER

HEIGHT:	**WEIGHT:**
5 FEET 11 INCHES (180 CM)	200 POUNDS (91 KG)

AMATEUR TEAM:
RIMOUSKI OCEANIC
QUEBEC MAJOR JUNIOR
HOCKEY LEAGUE

NHL TEAM:
PITTSBURGH PENGUINS

Sports Illustrated KIDS

 LEGENDS IN THE MAKING

HOCKEY LEGENDS IN THE MAKING

BY SHANE FREDERICK

CAPSTONE PRESS
a capstone imprint

Sports Illustrated Kids Legends in the Making are published by Capstone Press,
1710 Roe Crest Drive, North Mankato, Minnesota 56003
www.capstonepub.com

Library of Congress Cataloging-in-Publication Data
Frederick, Shane.
  Hockey legends in the making / by Shane Frederick.
     pages cm.—(Sports illustrated kids. Legends in the making)
  Includes index.
  ISBN 978-1-4765-4065-8 (library binding)
  ISBN 978-1-4765-5191-3 (paperback)
1. Hockey players—Biography—Juvenile literature. I. Title.
  GV848.5.A1F74 2014
  796.9620922—dc23   2013032772

Editorial Credits
Anthony Wacholtz, editor; Ted Williams, set designer; Terri Poburka, designer;
     Eric Gohl, media researcher; Jennifer Walker, production specialist

Photo Credits
Newscom/ZUMA Press: Debby Wong, 24, Matthew Manor, 11; Shutterstock: mexrix,
1; *Sports Illustrated*: Bob Rosato, 23, Damian Strohmeyer, cover (bottom right), 8, 10–11
(bkg), 15, 18–19 (bkg), 19, 22–23 (bkg), 31 (bottom), David E. Klutho, cover (bottom
left), 4, 4–5 (bkg), 8–9 (bkg), 12, 12–13 (bkg), 16, 16–17 (bkg), 24–25 (bkg), 26–27 (bkg),
27, 28, 30, 31 (top), Robert Beck, cover (top), 6–7 (bkg), 7, 20, 20–21 (bkg), 28–29 (bkg),
Simon Bruty, 14–15 (bkg)

Design Elements
Shutterstock

Printed in the United States of America in Stevens Point, Wisconsin.
092013   007768WZS14

When Sidney Crosby was just 19 years old, the Pittsburgh Penguins stitched the letter C on his jersey. He became the youngest **captain** in the history of the NHL at the time. A native of Cole Harbour, Nova Scotia, Crosby accomplished a lot more than that before he turned 20. He scored 120 points (36 goals, 84 assists) in 2006–07. The total made him the first teenager to lead the league in scoring and the youngest scoring champion in any North American sport.

Crosby continued to get better from there. "Sid the Kid" led the Penguins to a Stanley Cup championship in 2009. The next season he led the NHL in goals. He also scored the game-winning goal in **overtime** to clinch an Olympic gold medal for Canada in 2010. Injuries shortened his next two seasons, but Crosby returned to form in 2013. He finished third in the league in points.

Did You Know?

During his first five years in the NHL, Crosby lived at the home of Penguins owner and former superstar Mario Lemieux.

CAPTAIN—the leader of a sports team

OVERTIME—an extra period played if the score is tied at the end of regulation

Drew Doughty grew up in Ontario, Canada, home to two NHL teams. But his favorite team, the Kings, played far away in Los Angeles. His favorite player was the Great One, Wayne Gretzky, who spent more than seven years with the Kings. Doughty ended up playing for his favorite team after being **drafted** by Los Angeles in 2008. The Kings selected him with the second overall pick.

Doughty may be a defenseman, but he has proven to be one of the league's best players at both ends of the ice. He showed off those skills during the 2012 Stanley Cup Finals. He chased down a loose puck at one end of the rink before turning around. Then he carried it through three New Jersey Devils defensemen and netted a goal. With Doughty leading the way, Los Angeles won its first Stanley Cup.

Did You Know?

Doughty's other favorite sport is soccer. As a kid, he was a goalkeeper in a youth league.

DRAFT—to select a player to join a sports organization or team

DREW DOUGHTY

POSITION:
DEFENSEMAN

HEIGHT:	WEIGHT:
6 FEET 1 INCH (185 CM)	208 POUNDS (94 KG)

AMATEUR TEAM:
GUELPH STORM
ONTARIO HOCKEY LEAGUE

NHL TEAM:
LOS ANGELES KINGS

CLAUDE GIROUX

POSITION:

RIGHT WING

HEIGHT:	WEIGHT:
5 FEET 11 INCHES (180 CM)	172 POUNDS (78 KG)

AMATEUR TEAM:
GATINEAU OLYMPIQUES
QUEBEC MAJOR JUNIOR
HOCKEY LEAGUE

NHL TEAM:
PHILADELPHIA FLYERS

When the Philadelphia Flyers picked Claude Giroux during the first round of the 2006 draft, general manager Bobby Clarke briefly forgot Giroux's name. The crowd in the Vancouver, British Columbia, arena laughed at Clarke's mistake. No one can forget Giroux's name now.

Giroux made his Flyers debut two years later and continued to get better. During the 2010 Stanley Cup playoffs, Giroux scored 21 points in 23 games before the Flyers fell to the Blackhawks in the Finals. Two years later Giroux had another amazing playoff performance. In a single game, he scored six points (three goals, three assists) in a victory over the Penguins. In 2013 he was named the Flyers' captain.

⤵ Did You Know?

Giroux has a ritual of eating a grilled-cheese sandwich before every game.

The 2011 All-Star break was coming up, and Erik Karlsson had arranged to get away for the weekend. But then he got some news that forced him to change his plans. At just 20 years old, Karlsson had been selected to play in the **midseason classic**.

The native of Landsbro, Sweden, was picked by the Ottawa Senators in the first round of the 2008 draft. He quickly proved to be one of the league's best offensive defensemen. In 2011–12 he led all **blueliners** with 78 points (19 goals, 59 assists). He earned the Norris Trophy as the NHL's best defenseman. Only Bruins great Bobby Orr was younger when he won the award.

Did You Know?

Karlsson was the second Swedish player to win the Norris Trophy. The first was the Red Wings' Nicklas Lidstrom, who won it seven times.

MIDSEASON CLASSIC—another name for the All-Star Game

BLUELINER—a nickname for a defenseman; defensemen often play near the rink's blue lines

ERIK KARLSSON

POSITION:
DEFENSEMAN

HEIGHT:	WEIGHT:
6 FEET (183 CM)	175 POUNDS (79 KG)

PREVIOUS TEAM:
FROLUNDA HC
GOTEBORG, SWEDEN

NHL TEAM:
OTTAWA SENATORS

EVGENI MALKIN

POSITION:

CENTER

HEIGHT:	WEIGHT:
6 FEET 3 INCHES (191 CM)	195 POUNDS (88 KG)

PREVIOUS TEAM:
METALLURG MAGNITOGORSK KONTINENTAL HOCKEY LEAGUE, RUSSIA

NHL TEAM:
PITTSBURGH PENGUINS

To say that Evgeni Malkin burst on the scene might be an understatement. The tall 20-year-old **rookie** from Russia scored a goal in each of his first six games for the Pittsburgh Penguins. It was a feat that hadn't been accomplished since 1917—nearly 90 years earlier.

Malkin, who began playing professional hockey in his hometown when he was 17 years old, didn't stop there. In 2009 he led the NHL in scoring with 113 points (35 goals, 78 assists). That season the Penguins won the Stanley Cup. Malkin became the first Russian to win the Conn Smythe Trophy as playoff **MVP**. He won the Hart Trophy as league MVP in 2012.

Did You Know?

Malkin's father, Vladimir, also played professional hockey for Metallurg Magnitogorsk in Russia.

ROOKIE—a first-year player

MVP—an honor given to the best player each season; MVP stands for most valuable player

"The Goal" might be the defining moment of Alex Ovechkin's high-scoring young career. The Washington Capitals winger burst into the offensive zone and tried to skate around one last Phoenix Coyotes player. But the defenseman stood him up with a body check and knocked him down. As he fell to the ice, Ovechkin reached back for the puck. With his back to the goal, he **backhanded** the puck into the net for an amazing goal.

A year earlier, in 2005–06, Ovechkin won the Calder Trophy as the NHL's rookie of the year. In 2007–08 he scored 65 goals and won the Hart Trophy as league MVP. Ovechkin has led the NHL in goals three times.

Did You Know?

Alex Ovechkin's mother, Tatyana, was an Olympic basketball player. She won gold medals with the Soviet Union in 1976 and 1980.

BACKHAND—to shoot or pass the puck using the back side of the stick's blade

ALEX OVECHKIN

POSITION:
LEFT WING

HEIGHT:	WEIGHT:
6 FEET 3 INCHES (191 CM)	230 POUNDS (104 KG)

PREVIOUS TEAM:
DYNAMO MOSCOW
RUSSIA

NHL TEAM:
WASHINGTON CAPITALS

ZACH PARISE

POSITION:

LEFT WING

HEIGHT:	WEIGHT:
5 FEET 11 INCHES (180 CM)	190 POUNDS (86 KG)

COLLEGE TEAM:

UNIVERSITY OF NORTH DAKOTA

// **NHL TEAMS:**
NEW JERSEY DEVILS, MINNESOTA WILD

Zach Parise practically grew up in a hockey rink. His dad, J.P. Parise, played nine seasons for the Minnesota North Stars and was later an assistant coach with the team. Zach often watched practices run by his dad and learned to skate in the arena where the North Stars played.

Parise was drafted in the first round by the New Jersey Devils in 2003. He played seven seasons there following an All-American season at the University of North Dakota. He became known as one of the league's hardest workers and went to the All-Star Game in 2009. In 2012 he led the Devils to the Stanley Cup Finals. The following year Parise decided to return to the place where he started skating and joined the Minnesota Wild.

Did You Know?

Parise wears number 11 for the Wild, the same number his father wore for the North Stars.

Anahim Lake, British Columbia, wasn't an ideal spot for a future NHL goalie to grow up. Getting to practices and games meant a six-hour round-trip drive for Carey Price's family. Eventually his dad decided to get his pilot's license and fly 10-year-old Carey to the rink.

All of that travel paid off in 2005, when the Montreal Canadiens drafted Price with the fifth overall pick. Some goaltenders take years to develop into professional players, but not Price. He won 24 NHL games and had three shutouts as a 20-year-old rookie. Three seasons later he played in 72 games and led the league with 38 wins. That season he also became the seventh-youngest goalie in NHL history to win 100 career games.

⤶ Did You Know?

Price's mother, Lynda, is a former chief of the Ulkatcho First Nation in British Columbia, Canada.

CAREY PRICE

POSITION:
GOALTENDER

HEIGHT:	WEIGHT:
6 FEET 3 INCHES (191 CM)	209 POUNDS (95 KG)

AMATEUR TEAM:
TRI-CITY AMERICANS
WESTERN HOCKEY LEAGUE

NHL TEAM:
MONTREAL CANADIENS

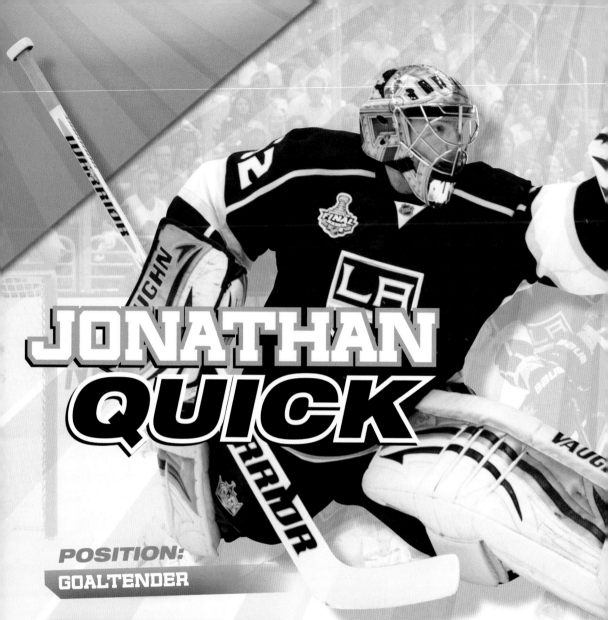

JONATHAN QUICK

POSITION:
GOALTENDER

HEIGHT:	WEIGHT:
6 FEET 1 INCH (185 CM)	218 POUNDS (99 KG)

COLLEGE TEAM:
UNIVERSITY OF MASSACHUSETTS

NHL TEAM:
LOS ANGELES KINGS

During the 2012 Stanley Cup Finals, Los Angeles Kings goalie Jonathan Quick amazed even his teammates. The eighth goaltender picked in the 2005 draft, Quick strung together one of the best playoff runs by a goalie in NHL history. He led the Kings to their first championship by going 16-4 in the **postseason**. He stopped 94.6 percent of opponents' shots, giving up 1.41 goals per game. In six games against the New Jersey Devils in the finals, Quick allowed only six goals. As a result, he became just the third American-born player to win the Conn Smythe Trophy as playoff MVP.

Did You Know?

Quick has pulled off a rare feat twice—once in college and once in the minor leagues. The goalie was credited with scoring a goal by being the last player from his team to touch the puck before it went in the opponents' net.

POSTSEASON—the Stanley Cup playoffs; the postseason is played after the regular season

MINOR LEAGUES—a level of professional play below the NHL

Drafted with the first overall pick in 2008, Steven Stamkos didn't get off to the best start with the Tampa Bay Lightning. In his first 16 professional games, Stamkos scored just one goal. His coach, Barry Melrose, said the rookie wasn't ready for the NHL. Stamkos quickly proved him wrong.

The Markham, Ontario, native became one of the league's best goal scorers that year. He ended up with 23 goals as a rookie. The following year he tied Sidney Crosby for the most goals with 51. Two years later Stamkos held the goal-scoring title by himself with an impressive 60 goals. That number included an NHL-record five overtime winners.

➛ Did You Know?

Stamkos' first job was selling steaks at the St. Lawrence Market in Toronto, Ontario.

STEVEN STAMKOS

POSITION:

CENTER

HEIGHT:	WEIGHT:
6 FEET (183 CM)	190 POUNDS (86 KG)

AMATEUR TEAM:
SARNIA STING
ONTARIO HOCKEY LEAGUE

// **NHL TEAM:**
TAMPA BAY LIGHTNING

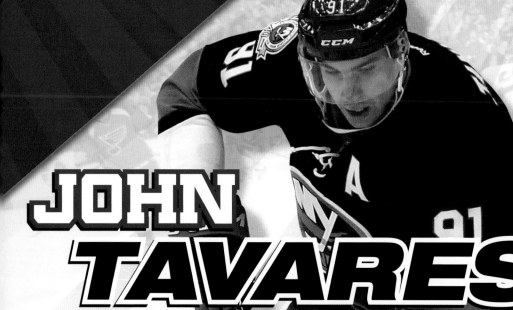

JOHN TAVARES

POSITION:
CENTER

HEIGHT:	WEIGHT:
6 FEET	199 POUNDS
(183 CM)	(90 KG)

AMATEUR TEAM:
LONDON KNIGHTS/
OSHAWA GENERALS
ONTARIO HOCKEY LEAGUE

NHL TEAM:
NEW YORK ISLANDERS

John Tavares has always played at a higher level than most players his age. When he was just 14 years old, he became the youngest player drafted into the Ontario Hockey League. At age 16 he scored 72 goals in the OHL, breaking an age-group record set by the great Wayne Gretzky. Tavares set a career record in the OHL with 215 goals.

The New York Islanders drafted Tavares with the first overall pick in 2009. The Mississauga, Ontario, native continued to score. He had 24 goals and 54 points as a rookie. He increased his point total to 67 and 81 over the next two seasons. In 2012–13 Tavares was a **candidate** for the Hart Trophy as league MVP.

Did You Know?

Tavares is the godfather of Mila, the daughter of teammate and longtime friend Matt Moulson.

CANDIDATE—a person being considered for an award

Coaches and teammates began raving about Jonathan Toews' leadership when the center was a 19-year-old rookie. A year later the Chicago Blackhawks named him captain. That honor made Toews the third-youngest captain in NHL history at the time. He turned out to be the right man for the job.

The third overall draft pick in 2006, the Winnipeg, Manitoba, native made an immediate impact in Chicago, scoring a point in each of his first 10 games. It was the second-longest streak of its kind to start a career. In his third season, Toews led the Blackhawks to their first Stanley Cup championship in 49 years. After scoring 29 points in 22 postseason games that year, he won the Conn Smythe Trophy as playoff MVP. In 2013 Toews became the second player in NHL history to captain two Stanley Cup championship teams by age 25. The legendary Wayne Gretzky was the first.

Did You Know?

In 2007 Toews played for Team Canada, which won the gold medal at the International Ice Hockey Federation World Championships.

JONATHAN TOEWS

POSITION:

CENTER

HEIGHT:	WEIGHT:
6 FEET 2 INCHES (188 CM)	208 POUNDS (94 KG)

COLLEGE TEAM:
UNIVERSITY OF NORTH DAKOTA

// NHL TEAM:
CHICAGO BLACKHAWKS

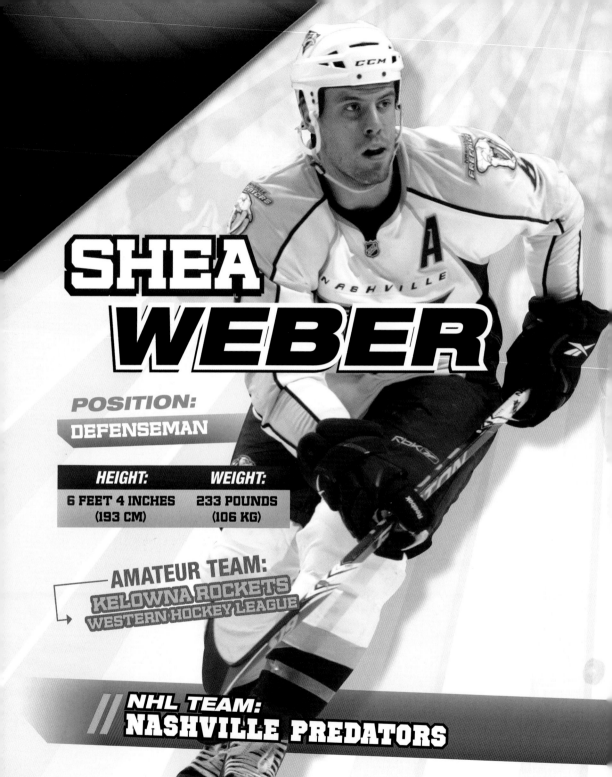

SHEA
WEBER

POSITION:

DEFENSEMAN

HEIGHT:	WEIGHT:
6 FEET 4 INCHES (193 CM)	233 POUNDS (106 KG)

AMATEUR TEAM:
KELOWNA ROCKETS
WESTERN HOCKEY LEAGUE

NHL TEAM:
NASHVILLE PREDATORS

After the 2011–12 season, the Philadelphia Flyers made a 14-year, $110 million offer to Shea Weber. The Nashville Predators, the team Weber played with for his first seven seasons, had no choice but to match it to keep him.

Weber is an **elite** defenseman who also can score goals. His slap shot can reach 103 miles (166 kilometers) per hour, and he can rack up points on the **power play**. He is a rugged player who can block shots and knock down the NHL's best forwards. He's a player who rarely comes off the ice, averaging more than 26 minutes per game.

Did You Know?

Weber was the runner-up twice for the Norris Trophy as the NHL's best defenseman.

ELITE—describes players who are among the best in the league

POWER PLAY—when one team has more players on the ice because the other team has one or more players in the penalty box

RISING STARS

GABRIEL LANDESKOG

The Colorado Avalanche took Landeskog with the second overall draft pick in 2011. The left wing won the Calder Trophy as rookie of the year after the 2011–12 season. He played in every game that season, scoring 22 goals and 52 points.

ALEX PIETRANGELO

It didn't take long for the fourth overall draft pick in 2008 to become the St. Louis Blues' best defenseman. He's the youngest player in team history to score 40 points in back-to-back seasons.

TUUKKA RASK

Rask went from reserve to replacing Stanley Cup hero Tim Thomas as the Boston Bruins' starting goalie when he was 25 years old.

RYAN NUGENT-HOPKINS

The center was just 18 years old when he played his first NHL game for the Edmonton Oilers. The first overall pick in 2011 scored 52 points in his first season, including the first five-assist game by an 18-year-old.

TYLER SEGUIN

At age 20 Seguin became the youngest player in Boston Bruins' history to lead the team in scoring (67 points). A year earlier he helped Boston win the Stanley Cup. After the 2012–13 season, Seguin was traded to the Dallas Stars.

READ MORE

Frederick, Shane. *The Best of Everything Hockey Book.*
Sports Illustrated Kids. Mankato, Minn.: Capstone Press, 2011.

Gitlin, Martin. *The Stanley Cup: All About Pro Hockey's Biggest Event.*
Sports Illustrated Kids. Mankato, Minn.: Capstone Press, 2013.

Roza, Greg. *Sidney Crosby.* New York: Gareth Stevens Pub., 2012.

Savage, Jeff. *Alex Ovechkin.* Minneapolis: Lerner Publications Co., 2012.

INTERNET SITES

FactHound offers a safe, fun way to find Internet sites
related to this book. All of the sites on FactHound
have been researched by our staff.

Here's all you do:

Visit *www.facthound.com*

Type in this code: 9781476540658

Super-cool stuff! Check out projects, games and lots more at
www.capstonekids.com

INDEX

All-Star Games, 10, 17
awards, 10, 13, 14, 21, 25, 26, 29, 30
centers, 5, 13, 22, 25, 26, 31
defensemen, 6, 10, 29, 30

drafts, 6, 9, 17, 18, 21, 22, 25, 26
goaltenders, 18, 21, 31
left wings, 14, 17, 30
playoffs, 6, 9, 13, 17, 21, 26, 31
right wings, 9

JUL 0 8 2014